Contents

KT-593-931

Food is fuel

A car needs petrol or diesel fuel to keep it running. A fire needs fuel, such as wood or coal, to keep it burning. Your body needs fuel, too. Food is the body's fuel.

▲
Without fuel a car will not work. When the fuel burns it gives out energy that powers the engine.

Giving energy

We need food for energy. Everything we do needs energy. Things such as running or cycling use a lot of energy. Breathing, keeping the heart beating, and even thinking also use energy. All this energy comes from food.

When we are doing something active, such as football, we need more energy than if we are resting.

▼

Food and Digestion

Andrew Solway

Franklin Watts
338 Euston Road
London NW1 3BH

Franklin Watts Australia
Level 17/207 Kent Street
Sydney, NSW 2000

Series editor: Sarah Peutrill
Design: Mo Choy
Cover design: Peter Scoulding
Photographer: Paul Bricknell, unless otherwise stated
Illustrations: Ian Thompson
Consultant: Peter Riley

Picture credits: Matt Apps/Shutterstock: 7t. Andrea
Comas/Reuters/Corbis: 11. Andy Crawford: 14, 19b. Elena
Elisseeva/Shutterstock: 29. Eye of Science/SPL: 22.
Hannamariah/Shutterstock: 27. Sebastian Knight/Shutterstock: 5t. Ray
Moller/Franklin Watts: 28. Professors P. Motta & F.Carpino/University "La
Sapienza", Rome/SPL: 25t. Amy Myers/Shutterstock: 4b. John Radcliffe
Hospital, Oxford/SPL: 26t. Franziska Richter/Shutterstock: 4t

Every attempt has been made to clear copyright. Should there be any
inadvertent omission please apply to the publisher for rectification.

With thanks to our models: Isabella Chang-leng, Chay Harrison, Liam
Lane, Charlie Pitt, Kate Polley, Eoin Serle, Marcel Yearwood.

A CIP catalogue record for this book is available from the British Library.

Dewey number: 612.3
ISBN: 978 1 4451 3882 4
Printed in China

Franklin Watts is a division of Hachette Children's Books,
an Hachette UK company.
www.hachette.co.uk

Growth and repair

We need food to grow and repair our bodies. Whenever we are growing fast, we need more food. Throughout our lives, our bodies constantly have to repair general wear and tear. Our skin, for instance, is continually being worn away, and new skin grows to replace it. Sometimes we get cuts and scrapes that need repairing as well. The food we eat helps us do all this.

▲
When we get a cut or a graze, the body has to make new skin and other tissue. This takes energy.

◀ A car runs on one kind of fuel. However, we need to eat a variety of different foods.

Water

Water is very important for our bodies too! Our bodies are made of about 65% of water!

Energy foods: starches

Our bodies do not work on just one kind of fuel. We need to eat a variety of different foods. Each kind of food contains a mixture of nutrients. These are substances the body needs to make it work properly.

Carbohydrates

Some foods are rich in one kind of nutrient. For instance, bread, rice, pasta and potatoes are rich in starch. Starch is an energy food. The body can break down starch to generate energy. Starch is one of a group of nutrients called carbohydrates. They are the most important part of our diet. We need more carbohydrates than any other kind of food.

Starchy foods such as pasta release their energy slowly. They keep us going for several hours.

▼

Super starch

Starch is the most common kind of carbohydrate. Over half of all the carbohydrate we eat is starch.

Fibre

Foods such as wholewheat bread and brown rice are rich in another kind of carbohydrate called fibre. A lot of fibre is material that we cannot digest (break down into nutrients). This kind of fibre helps the digestive system to work properly (see page 24). Other kinds of fibre help our bodies to get a steady supply of energy and help to protect us against heart disease.

▲ Athletes in long-distance races such as marathons need large energy reserves to get through a race. They 'load up' with starchy foods two or three days before the event.

Foods such as porridge ▶ and wholewheat bread are rich in fibre, which helps us digest our food.

Energy foods: sugars

Biscuits, sweets, chocolate and honey all contain large amounts of another carbohydrate called sugar. Like starch, sugar gives you energy.

Sugary foods such ▶ as honey, biscuits and sweets are very nice to eat. But too much sugar is bad for you.

Different kinds

There are several kinds of sugar. The kind in your sugar bowl is called sucrose. Honey is mostly a sugar called fructose. The main sugar in milk is lactose. Another sugar, called glucose, circulates in our blood. It is the main nutrient that we use for energy.

Don't eat too much sugar

It is not good to eat too many sugary foods, for two main reasons. First, our bodies can use sugars quickly. The sugar gives you a short burst of energy, then you feel hungry again.

The second problem with sugary foods is that they can damage your teeth. If you want to avoid painful tooth decay, it is best to have sugary foods only as an occasional treat.

Tooth decay

Tooth decay is caused by microscopic germs called bacteria that live on your teeth. When you eat, tiny bits of food get stuck between your teeth. These bits of food, especially sugary foods, feed billions of bacteria. The bacteria produce acids that eat away the surface of the tooth itself.

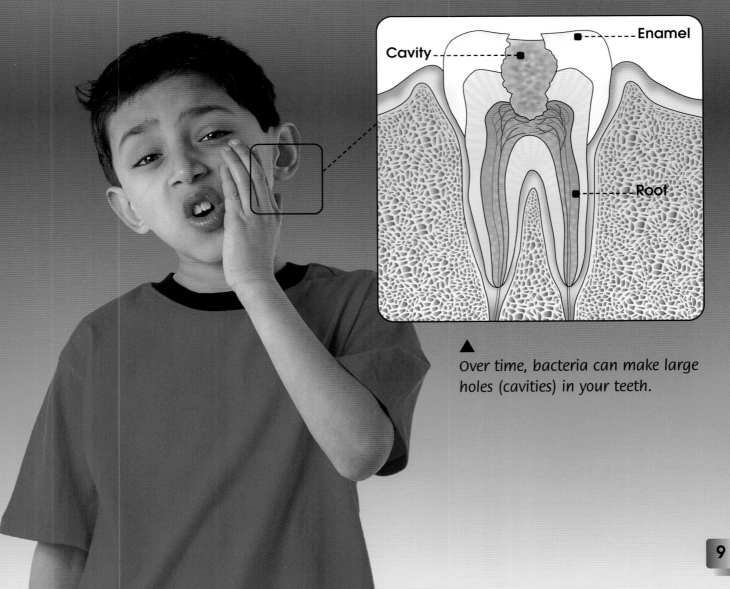

▲
Over time, bacteria can make large holes (cavities) in your teeth.

Body-building foods

Foods such as lean meat, fish, chicken, cheese, beans and nuts are rich in proteins. Proteins are body-building foods.

The proteins in muscles can contract (shorten). This makes them pull on our bones, which allows us to move.
▼

Growth and repair
We need proteins for the body to grow and repair itself. One reason for this is that a lot of the body is made of protein. Our muscles are mostly protein, and protein is an important part of bones. Our hair and nails are also made of protein.

Hair

Nails

Muscle

Bone

Growth spurts

Young babies need to eat foods containing protein as most of them almost triple in size in their first year. Teenagers also grow fast, which explains why they eat so much! Women who are pregnant need extra food to help the baby inside them grow.

Chemical reactions

Proteins have another important job in the body – they make everything work! Every moment, there are thousands of chemical reactions going on inside our bodies. Without these reactions, the body would not work. Proteins called enzymes make these reactions happen.

When a weightlifter is in ▶ training for a competition, she eats a high-protein diet. The extra protein helps to build up her muscles.

Fats and oils

Fried eggs, crisps and ice cream are foods rich in fat. Fats and oils are another food we need in our diet.

Cells, the brain and warmth

Some very important parts of the body are made from fats. The whole of the body is made up of microscopic parts called cells. Each cell is separated from its neighbours by a thin membrane. These membranes are made mostly of fat. We need fats for other things, too. They help the brain develop, and a layer of special fat under our skin helps to keep us warm.

◀ Fat, as in this doughnut, is a concentrated energy food. We only need fairly small amounts of fat to stay healthy.

Brown fat

Many animals have a layer of fat to help them stay warm. However, young babies have a different kind of fat, called brown fat. Young babies can easily get cold, because they are so small. The brown fat tissue can produce heat, which helps protect them in cold weather.

Energy food

Fat is also energy food. In fact, there is more energy in fatty food than in carbohydrates. However, our bodies do not use fat for instant energy. Fats are a way to store spare energy. This is why, if we eat too much fatty food, we become overweight.

Brain

▲
Fats are very important for building your brain. About two-thirds of the brain is fat.

Fruit and vegetables

Why is it so important to eat at least five portions of fruit and vegetables a day? One reason is that fruit and vegetables are a good source of vitamins and minerals, which our bodies need.

Minerals

Minerals are simple substances that we need in small amounts. Iron, calcium and magnesium are examples of minerals. Iron is an important part of the blood, while we need calcium for strong bones. Magnesium helps your body to fight germs.

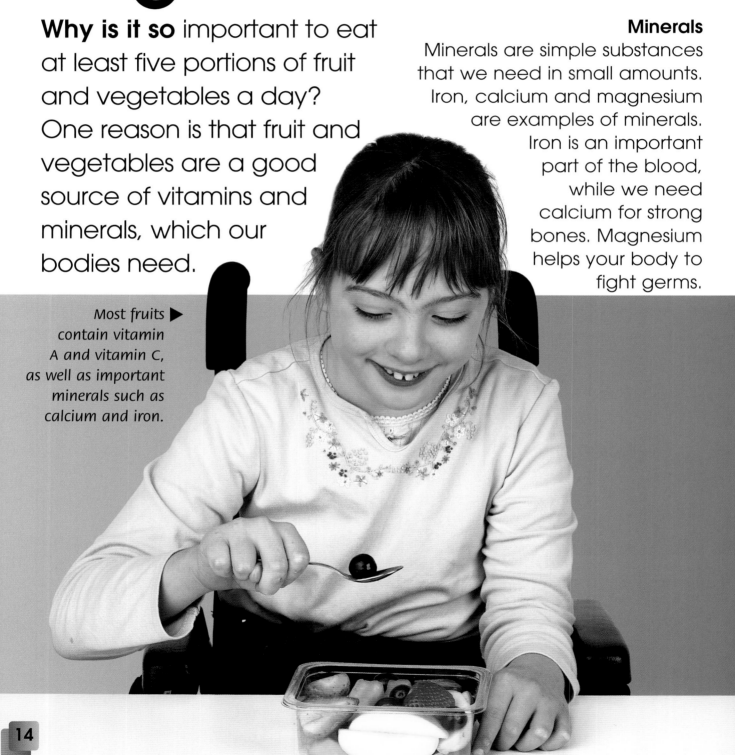

Most fruits ▶ contain vitamin A and vitamin C, as well as important minerals such as calcium and iron.

Vitamins

We need vitamins in even smaller amounts than we need minerals. Even so, vitamins are essential for us to be healthy. Vitamin C is the best known vitamin. It has many important jobs. It helps fight off disease, and we need it to absorb iron into the body.

In our bones, living tissues are surrounded by a tough, hard material. The hard part of the bones is mainly calcium.
▼

Scurvy!

For many years, sailors on long sea voyages suffered from a disease called scurvy. Their skin developed large spots, their teeth became loose and their gums bled. Scurvy is caused by a lack of vitamin C. In the 1750s a Scottish sea-captain called James Lind found that lemon juice cured scurvy. Soon afterwards the British Navy began giving sailors lemons or limes on all long voyages.

What happens to food?

Once we eat it, food has to go through many processes before the body can use it for energy, growth and repair.

Our digestive system

The body has several parts that specialise in taking, breaking down and absorbing food. All these parts together are called the digestive system. Our food's journey begins in the mouth, then goes to the digestive tube, or gut, which is a long tube that runs right through the body. Together with other organs this forms the digestive system.

Secret muscles

The walls of the gut are full of muscles. The muscles contract (shorten) and relax to push food along the gut. If you swallow, you can feel the muscles working in your oesophagus (the tube leading to your stomach). But you can't feel the muscles in the rest of your gut, or make them work. They work automatically, without you knowing about it.

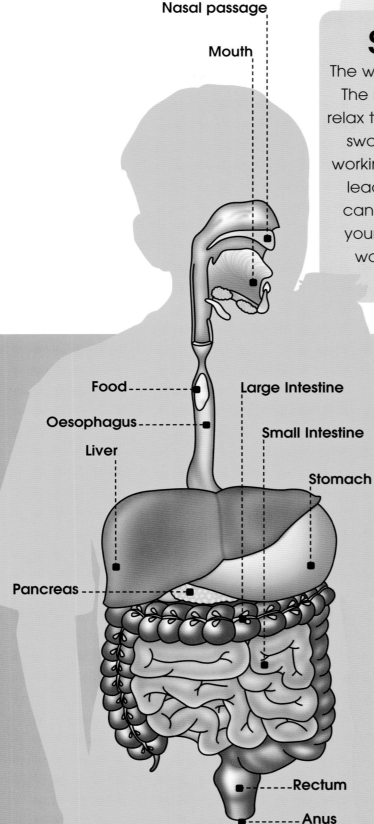

Nasal passage

Mouth

Food

Oesophagus

Liver

Pancreas

Large Intestine

Small Intestine

Stomach

Rectum

Anus

In and out

Food cannot be absorbed into the body as it is. The digestive system takes the carbohydrates, proteins and fats from our food and breaks them down into simpler nutrients. Some of the food we eat is waste material that our bodies cannot use. This goes right through the body and comes out of the anus (bottom).

◀ *Our digestive system is a long tube that winds through the body. If it was laid out straight, it would be about 10 metres long.*

Chew and swallow

The first stage of digestion happens in your mouth. The mouth can deal with all kinds of food, whether they are hard or soft, cooked or raw.

Teeth and saliva

As you chomp on your food, your teeth break it up into smaller pieces. The saliva (spit) in your mouth helps too, by softening the food up. Once you have chewed your food, you swallow it.

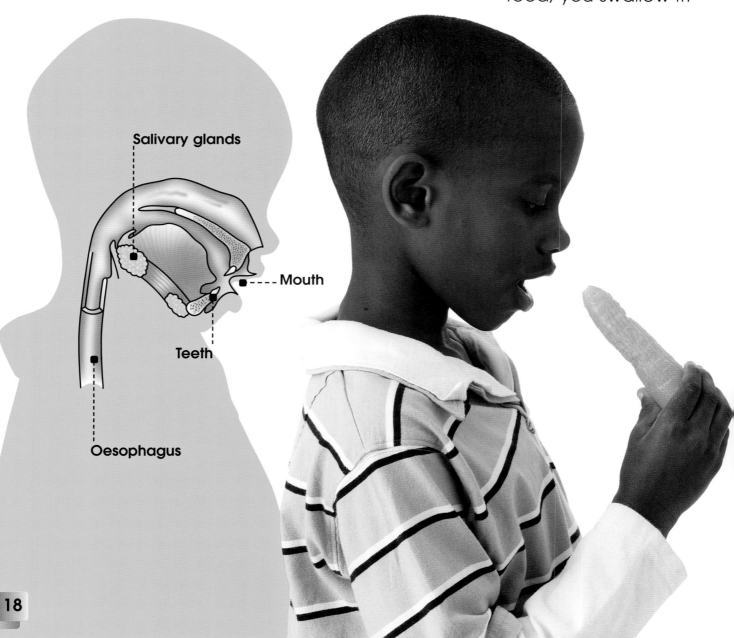

Salivary glands

Mouth

Teeth

Oesophagus

Down the oesophagus

The tube from your mouth to your stomach is called the oesophagus. The muscles in the oesophagus push the food down. At the bottom is a ring of muscle that acts like a valve. It lets food into the stomach, but doesn't let it back up again.

In the stomach

The stomach is like a large bag with thick, muscular walls. The stomach walls squash the food and churn it about. The stomach also adds special juices to the food. These start to break down the carbohydrates and proteins.

When empty, the stomach is no larger than a fist, but when full it can grow up to 20 times bigger.
▼

▲
We can eat and drink even if we are upside down. This is because muscles in the oesophagus push the food or drink into the stomach.

Strong acid

The stomach juices are acid. If you got stomach juice on your hand, it could burn your skin! The lining of the stomach is protected from this acid by a thick, gooey liquid called mucus. This mucus stops the acid from burning the stomach walls.

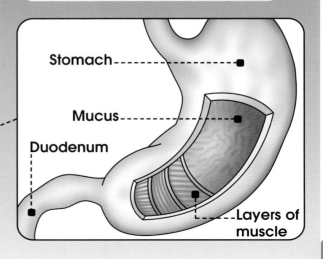

Stomach

Mucus

Duodenum

Layers of muscle

Into the intestines

From the stomach, food goes into a tube called the duodenum. This is the first part of a long section of the gut called the small intestine.

More digestive juices
In the duodenum, more digestive juices finish breaking down the food. The juices come from two organs, the pancreas and the gall bladder. The pancreas produces juices that can break down proteins, fats and starch.

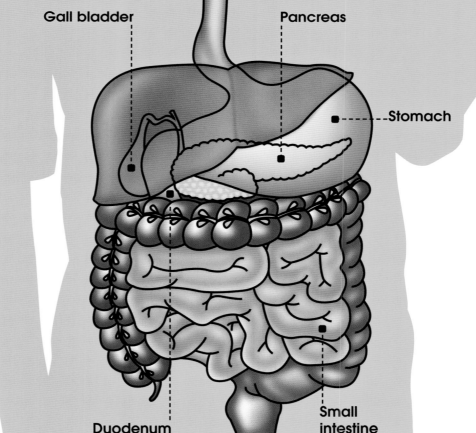

Gall bladder

Pancreas

Stomach

The pancreas and ▶ the gall bladder are close to the duodenum.

Duodenum

Small intestine

Amazing enzymes

The digestive juices from the pancreas contain many enzymes (see page 11). The enzymes speed up the chemical reactions that break down food. Enzymes speed up these processes an enormous amount. Some reactions go a billion times faster when there is an enzyme present!

The gall bladder

The gall bladder produces a green liquid called bile. This does two main jobs. First, it breaks up blobs of fat into droplets that can be broken down much more quickly. Second, the bile neutralises the strong acid from the stomach. The lining of the intestine cannot stand acid in the same way as the stomach can. Without the bile, it would be damaged.

Separate layers

Shake it!

All mixed up

Try this!

A salad dressing is a mixture of fat and watery liquid (vinegar). Shake a bottle to see the fat break into tiny drops and mix with the vinegar. The bile helps this kind of mixing of fat and water in the duodenum.

Absorbing food

From the duodenum, the mixture of food and digestive juices moves further down the small intestine. This is the area where most food is absorbed.

Villi

The inside of the small intestine looks a bit like a pet's rubber brush. It is covered in very tiny, finger-like projections called villi. Each villus has blood vessels inside it. The villi provide a large surface area for absorbing nutrients into the blood.

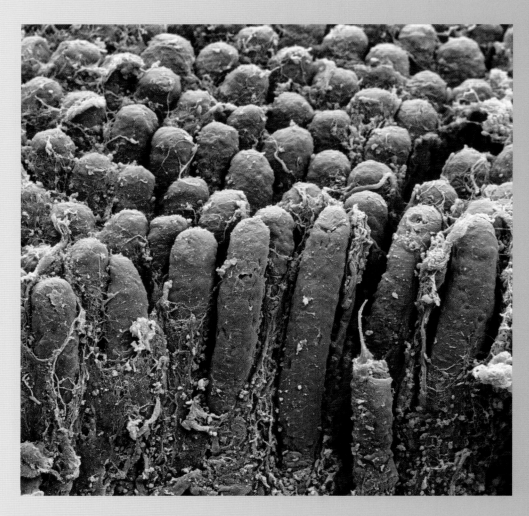

◀ This micrograph shows some of the millions of tiny villi inside the small intestine. The picture is enlarged 200 times.

Tardis intestines

In one way, the small intestine is like Dr Who's Tardis. It is much bigger on the inside than on the outside. If the insides of your intestines were spread out as a flat sheet, they would cover an area bigger than two tennis courts!

The liver

Once the nutrients are in the blood, they go to the liver. Your liver is like a combination of a warehouse and a chemical factory. It stores some nutrients to use later.

The liver turns other nutrients into useful substances for the body to use straight away. These are carried all around the body in the blood. Every cell in the body gets its nutrients from blood.

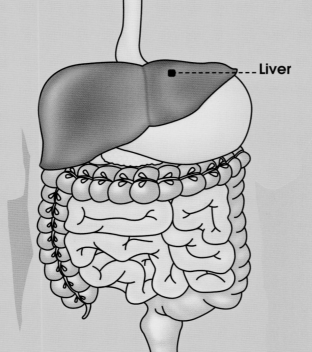

Liver

◀ *This picture shows the position of the liver in the body.*

Water and waste

By the end of the small intestine, most of the nutrients in your food have been absorbed. What is left is mostly waste, plus a lot of water.

Water
Altogether about 11 litres of liquid goes through your digestive system each day. The body cannot afford to lose so much water. Most of it is absorbed back into the body in the large intestine.

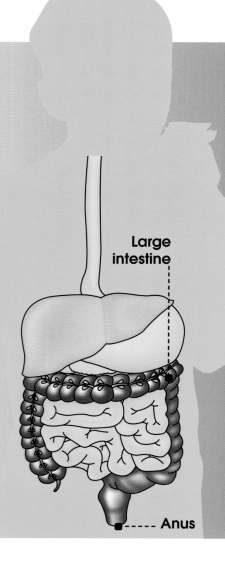

◀ *The main jobs of the large intestine are to absorb water and to get rid of waste material. It takes between one to three days from when you eat something for the undigested food to reach the anus.*

Large intestine

Anus

Helpful fibre
One thing that helps the large intestine to work well is plenty of fibre in your diet (see page 7). Fibre absorbs a lot of water, so it makes the waste food softer. This makes the waste pass through the large intestine more quickly and easily.

Bacteria

The large intestine is full of useful bacteria. They produce vitamin K and helps us absorb vitamins. Without vitamin K our blood would not clot when we bleed, and our bones would not grow properly.

Going out

The waste that is left at the end of the large intestine is called faeces (poo). When faeces reach the rectum you feel the urge to go to the toilet. Two rings of muscle around the anus relax and the faeces are pushed out.

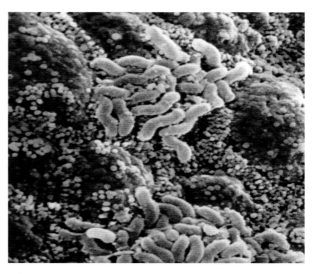

▲

The pink 'worms' in this micrograph are one kind of bacteria found in the large intestine. The picture is enlarged 200 times.

Wash your hands!

Over a third of the solid material in faeces is bacteria from the large intestine. Although they are useful in the large intestine, some of these bacteria can make us ill if they get anywhere else. This is why it is important to wash your hands after going to the toilet.

Problems with foods

Food is essential to life.
But foods can sometimes
cause people problems.

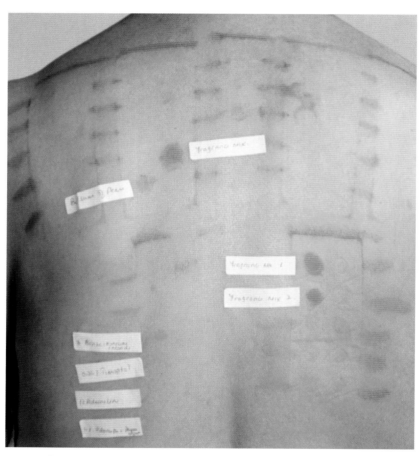

Some foods that cause allergies in some people:

Allergies

Some people are allergic
to certain foods. If they
eat these foods, they get
ill. There are seven main
foods that cause
allergies. They are milk,
eggs, nuts, fish, shellfish,
soya beans and wheat.

A food allergy might
just bring a person out
in a rash. However, some
people have much worse
reactions. They might be
sick, have muscle cramps
and have difficulty
breathing.

◀ *If you have an allergy, it can be
difficult to know what is causing
it. A doctor may carry out a
patch test like this to try and
find out what substance
is causing the problem.*

Milk

Eggs

Peanuts

Fish

Prawns

Bread (wheat)

Hidden in the label

Many pre-packed foods have nuts, soya or milk in them. For instance, cereals, crackers, soups and tinned tuna often contain soya protein, which comes from soya beans. If you have a food allergy, it is important to check food labels carefully.

Overeating

In the developed countries of the world, another problem with food is that people can eat too much of it. If we eat too much, we become overweight.

For young people, being overweight makes it harder to enjoy sports and other activities and may lead to serious health problems when they are older. People who are overweight are more likely to have illnesses such as heart disease.

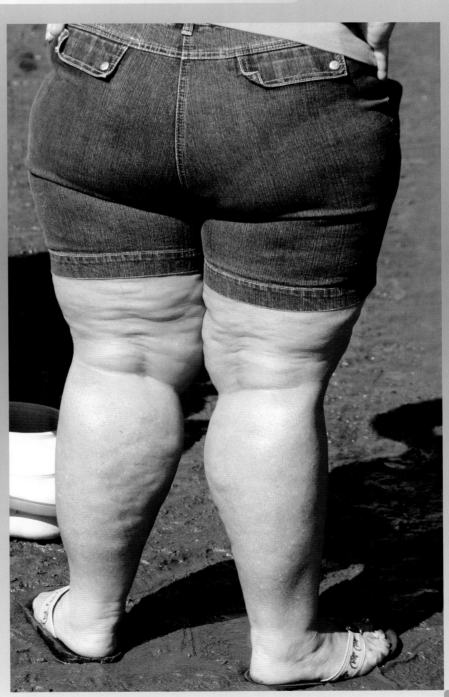

A person is 'obese' when ▶ *they have a very high, unhealthy amount of body fat. Obesity can lead to serious illnesses.*

A healthy diet

We need to eat a variety of different foods to be healthy. But what is a healthy diet?

A balanced meal is not just healthy – it's also really good to eat!
▼

The right balance

For a healthy diet we need to get the balance of foods right. We need plenty of carbohydrates for energy. These should be mainly starchy foods such as rice, pasta and potatoes. We also need to eat at least five portions of fruit and vegetables a day. This will give us important vitamins and minerals, and plenty of fibre.

Not too much

We should only have small amounts of sweet or fatty foods. Too much salt can also be bad for you. Foods such as crisps and takeaway foods are fatty and have lots of salt. If you eat a healthy diet when you are young, it will help keep you healthy and strong into old age.

Keeping active also helps us stay healthy. Doing sports, going swimming, cycling, walking, rollerblading and skateboarding are all good ways to keep fit.
▼

Strengthening bones

As we get older, our bones can begin to lose calcium. They become fragile and break easily. If we eat a good diet and exercise when we are younger, we build up the strength of our bones. We are less likely to have problems with our bones when we get older.

Glossary

absorb To take in something across body tissues, such as the skin, intestines, or kidneys.

acid A liquid that can make holes in solid things.

allergic If someone is allergic to a food, eating it gives them a rash or makes them ill.

bacteria Very simple, microscopic living things.

bile A green liquid produced by the gall bladder that helps to digest fat.

carbohydrates Foods such as starch and sugars, which give us energy.

cavities Holes in teeth caused by tooth decay.

cells Our whole body is made up of billions of very tiny cells.

clot A plug that forms at a wound to stop the body from bleeding.

cramp Painful soreness in a muscle.

diet Everything that we eat.

digestive system The parts of the body that digest (break down) food and get rid of waste.

duodenum The first part of the small intestine, where most of our food is digested.

enzymes Special proteins that speed up and control chemical reactions in the body.

faeces Poo – the waste that is left after digesting food.

fibre A food substance found in cereals, fruits and vegetables, which is not digested but helps the intestines to work properly.

gall bladder The organ where bile is stored.

iron A mineral that is essential to the body. Red meat and spinach provide a good source of iron in the diet.

micrograph A photograph taken through a microscope to show something many times bigger than it is.

minerals Simple chemicals such as iron and calcium, which we need in our diet.

nutrients Substances the body needs to make it work properly.

obesity When someone has above-normal body weight. It increases the risk for many health problems including heart disease.

oesophagus The tube that joins the mouth to the stomach.

pancreas The organ that produces most of the digestive juices that break down our food.

proteins Important foods that we need for growth and for repairing the body.

scurvy An illness caused by lack of vitamin C in the diet.

villi Tiny, finger-like projections on the inside of the small intestine.

vitamins Substances, such as vitamin C, that we need in our diet.

Further information
WEBSITES

www.bbc.co.uk/science/ humanbody/body gives you games and interactive information about the human body.

www.kidshealth.org gives you information about your body and healthy eating. Click on the section called 'for kids'.

Note to parents and teachers: Every effort has been made by the Publishers to ensure that these websites are suitable for children, that they are of the highest educational value, and that they contain no inappropriate or offensive material. However, because of the nature of the Internet, it is impossible to guarantee that the contents of these sites will not be altered. We strongly advise that Internet access is supervised by a responsible adult.

Index